Text: *Steve Goodier*
Series editor: *Tony Bowerman*
Photographs: *Steve Goodier, Steve Thompson/ www.sunstormphotography.com, Getty Images, National Trust Photo Library, Beatrix Potter Society, The Lingholm Estate/ www. thelingholmestate.co.uk , David Tarn/Cardtoons, Carl Rogers, Tony Bowerman, Shutterstock, Dreamstime*
Design: *Carl Rogers*

Northern Eye Books

ISBN 978-1-908632-19-7

A CIP catalogue record for this book is available from the British Library.

www.northerneyebooks.co.uk

Cover: *William Wordsworth and Beatrix Potter with one of their favourite places, Grasmere, in the background*

Important Advice: The routes described in this book are undertaken at the reader's own risk. Walkers should take into account their level of fitness, wear suitable footwear and clothing, and carry food and water. It is also advisable to take the relevant OS map with you in case you get lost and leave the area covered by our maps.

Whilst every care has been taken to ensure the accuracy of the route directions, the publisher cannot accept responsibility for errors or omissions, or for changes in the details given. Nor can the publisher and copyright owners accept responsibility for any consequences arising from the use of this book.

If you find any inaccuracies in either the text or maps, please write or email us at the address below. Thank you.

First published in 2014 by

Northern Eye Books Limited

Northern Eye Books, Tattenhall, Cheshire CH3 9PF
Email: tony@northerneyebooks.com

For sales enquiries, please call **01928 723 744**

Twitter: @top10walks | @northerneyeboo

Contents

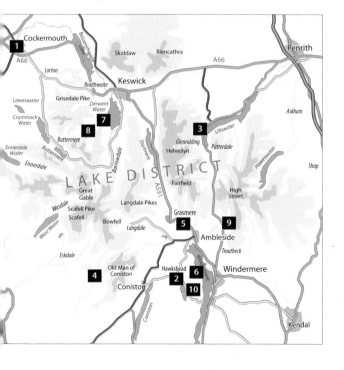

England's Largest National Park

THE LAKE DISTRICT NATIONAL PARK is the largest and most popular of the thirteen National Parks in England and Wales. Created as one of Britain's first National Parks in 1951, its role is to 'conserve and enhance' the natural beauty, wildlife and culture of this iconic English landscape, not just for residents and visitors today but for future generations, too.

Remarkably, the National Park contains every scrap of England's land over 3,000 feet, including its highest mountain, Scafell Pike. Packed within the Park's 885 square miles are numerous peaks and fells, over 400 lakes and tarns, around 50 dales, six National Nature Reserves, and more than 100 Sites of Special Scientific Interest—all publicly accessible on over 1,800 miles of footpaths and other rights of way. It's no surprise then, that the Lake District attracts an estimated 15 million visitors a year.

Derwentwater was a favourite of both William Wordsworth and Beatrix Potter

akeland's literary giants

he Lake District has a long history of literary residents:
ome native to the area and some 'off-comers' who
noved here in later life. Many of them also explored the
ea on foot and were bewitched by its timeless beauty.

William Wordsworth was a native of the Lakes, born at
ockermouth. **Beatrix Potter**, in contrast, came to live
ere inspired by memories of happy childhood holidays.

oth wrote prolifically and their names and works still
raw thousands of people to the Lake District each year
o see where they lived and the places and landscapes
ney loved. Now you can visit them, too.

"The Lake District… is a sort of national property in
which every man has a right and interest who has
an eye to perceive and a heart to enjoy."

William Wordsworth,
Guide Through the District of the Lakes in the North of England, 1810

TOP 10 **Walks:** Literary Walks

WILLIAM WORDSWORTH AND BEATRIX POTTER both lived long and active lives, and each had special places that were important to them. These carefully selected routes cover major points in their lives. In these ten walks you will explore lakes and tarns, walk through forests, and follow rough mountain track Some of the routes take you into remote terrain while others explore town paths and riverside paths. Yet all follow good paths and each walk has a clear relevance to these two much-loved and respected Lakeland authors.

'Wordsworth's birthplace' page 8

School days page 1

'Golden daffodils' page 20

'Favourite valley' page

LINGHOLM

PRIVATE

Wordsworth House, Cockermouth

William's birthplace

An easy, riverside walk around Cockermouth to visit Wordsworth House — birthplace of the famous poet

Distance/time: 5km/ 3 miles. Allow 2 hours (3½ hours if visiting Wordsworth House)

Start: Wakefield Road pay and display car park, Cockermouth

Grid ref: NY 117 309

Ordnance Survey Map: Explorer OL4 The English Lakes, North-western area: *Keswick, Cockermouth & Wigton*

After the walk: The Trout Hotel next to Wordsworth House. Crown Street, Cockermouth, CA13 0EJ. www.trouthotel.co.uk | 01900 823591| reservations@trouthotel.co.uk

Walk outline

The River Derwent is crossed via a bridge and we pass Wordsworth House picking up a riverside path, which is followed and left to walk through Jennings Brewery. The walk continues through Cockermouth, picking up the River Cocker which is followed before we climb into woodland. After crossing the Cocker higher up, we return via Harris Park and along roads and tracks. Wordsworth House is repassed at the end. For details, see: www.nationaltrust.org.uk/wordsworth-house

Wordsworth House

This is your chance to visit Wordsworth House in Cockermouth where William Wordsworth was born on 7th April 1770. His brothers Richard, John and Christopher, and his sister Dorothy, were born here too. The house was built in 1745 for Joshua Lucock, High Sheriff of Cumberland and bought in 1761 by Sir James Lowther. William's father, John, was the Lowthers' land agent and moved in with his wife, Anne, in 1766. When Anne died in 1778, the eight-year-old William was sent to live with relatives in Penrith. His father died at Wordsworth House in 1783.

Wordsworth's writing desk

Pen and poems

The Walk

1. Leave the car park via the exit signed for the 'Town Centre', towards the footbridge. Cross the bridge over the **River Derwent** and walk up **Bridge Street** to the junction with Cockermouth **High Street**. Turn right along the High Street and walk past **Wordsworth House**.

This is the house where William grew up 'Foster'd alike by beauty and by fear'. Now owned by the National Trust, the lovingly reconstructed Wordsworth House and Garden gives visitors the chance to experience at first hand the sights and sounds of 18th-century life. The Grade I

Listed Building is open to the public from March to October.

Immediately after Wordsworth House, turn right down **Low Sand Lane**, signed 'To the River'. At the end of the lane, bear right onto a path beside the **River Derwent**.

Wordsworth called the Derwent 'the fairest of all rivers' in the first book of his famous semi-autobiographical poem, 'The Prelude'.

2. Follow the path beneath the footbridge and between gardens and the river. Stay with the path as it curves right, between houses, to reach **Waterloo Street**. Turn left along the street, and, when this bends to the right, bear left over a footbridge across the **River Cocker** to reach **Brewery Lane**.

Brewery Lane is home to the Lake District's famous 'Jennings' Brewery which began life in Lorton Village in 1828. Jennings brew a range of local ales using Lakeland water drawn from their own well.

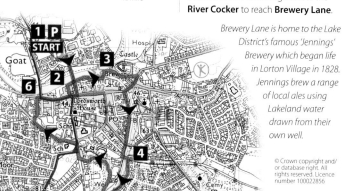

0 |————————————| 1km
  |————————————| ½ mile

Still glides the stream: *The footbridge over the Derwent just below Wordsworth House*

3. Curve right on Brewery Lane through the **Jennings Brewery.** Beyond the brewery, keep left, uphill to the end of the road. Turn right down **Castlegate,** crossing the bridge over the **River Cocker** near the **town centre**. Cross the road immediately after the river, and go through a **covered alleyway** between buildings. Walk through a small car park and turn left to the river. Bear right now with the river on your left, passing the **bowling club**. Continue beside the River Cocker to pass under a bridge.

The River Cocker rises at the head of the Buttermere Valley and flows for twelve miles before joining the River Derwent at Cockermouth. Its name is Celtic and means 'The Crooked One'.

Within 100 metres, immediately before the next high bridge over the river, go half-right, up a flight of wooden steps up an old railway embankment. They lead up to a **cycleway and footpath** along the trackbed of the disused railway.

Rivers' meet: *Cockermouth seen from the confluence of the Cocker and the Derwent*

4. Turn left over the bridge, then right almost immediately on a path signed 'Greenway'. The path weaves down through woods to reach playing fields. Go ahead, up the righthand edge of the **playing fields**, to reach a **footbridge** on the right. Cross the bridge and turn right into **Harris Park**.

Harris Park was given to Cockermouth in 1895 by the widow of Joseph Harris whose flax mill provided major employment for the people of the town. In 1896 Canon Rawnsley erected a bronze statue by a fountain (now gone) in memory of William and Dorothy Wordsworth. This was stolen but found in a Keswick garden. It has now been re-erected by the Wordsworth Memorial opposite Wordsworth House.

5. Walk through the park keeping ahead on the middle path. After a house on the right, bear left at the next junction. Pass a play area and leave the park through the **large gates** ahead. At the end of the road, turn right and continue downhill to go right at the next junction. Cross the road to the left at the traffic lights and continue ahead through the cycle barriers. Go through the car park and bear left towards **Kirklands Care Home**.

Turn right just before the care home car park along a 'footpath/cycleway'. Ignore a left, and at the end of the path go through another set of barriers onto a road. Head straight down **Horseman Street**.

6. Turn right and walk along the road to **Wordsworth House**. Cross over, turn right and retrace your outward route down Bridge Street to return to the car park and complete the walk. ♦

Cockermouth

Apart from William Wordsworth, Cockermouth's other famous resident was Fletcher Christian of 'Mutiny on The Bounty' notoriety. The town is so named because it is sited where the River Cocker flows into the River Derwent. Cockermouth is prone to flooding, having suffered damage in 2005 and, more recently and severely, on 19th November 2009. Wordsworth House has been flood damaged too but faithfully restored afterwards.

Hawkshead Grammar School, Wordsworth's old school

Wm. Wordsworth

School days

A circuit of Hawkshead where Wordsworth went to school, followed by a climb to the viewpoint of Latterbarrow

Distance/time: 7 kilometres/4 miles. Allow 2½ hours (or 3½ hours if visiting the Grammar School)

Start/finish: Hawkshead village pay and display car parks (toilets)

Grid ref: SD 352 980

Ordnance Survey Map: Explorer OL7 The English Lakes, South-eastern area: *Windermere, Kendal & Silverdale*

After the walk: The Kings Arms Hotel, Hawkshead, Ambleside, LA22 0NZ. www.kingsarmshawkshead.co.uk | 015394 36372 | info@kingsarmshawkeshead.co.uk

Walk outline

We start by visiting Hawkshead Grammar School and continue to St Michael's and All Angels Church. Next we take a look at Ann Tyson's house (where Wordsworth boarded) before following fields paths and tracks to climb a lane to the base of Latterbarrow. We climb steeply to the summit, following the ridge to drop back to the lane via woodland paths. The return to Hawkshead uses lanes, field paths and tracks. For school details, see: www.hawksheadgrammar.org.uk

Hawkshead Grammar School

During this walk you can visit the Grammar School attended by William Wordsworth. He had been taught to read by his mother but after her death in 1778 he was sent to live with relatives. He later went to Hawkshead where he lodged with Ann Tyson (whose house we also visit) and attended the village Grammar School from 1779-1787.

The school was founded in 1585 and downstairs you'll see original desks with carvings by pupils including William and his brother John. Upstairs there is an exhibition on the school and William Wordsworth.

Hawkshead church

Wordsworth's old school

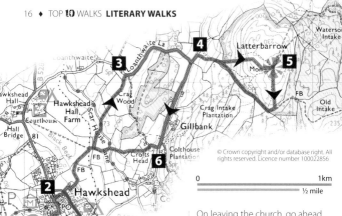

0   1km

        ½ mile

The Walk

1. Leave the car park and walk past the **toilets** towards the centre of the village.

The old **Grammar School** is directly ahead. Go through the gate and walk past the front of the school building and into the **churchyard**. Go right at a junction of paths and walk around to the entrance to **Hawkshead Church**.

Returning to Hawkshead from Cambridge in 1788, Wordsworth wrote in the Prelude: 'I saw the snow-white church upon her hill, Sit like a throned lady sending out, A gracious look all over her domain.' Now bare stone, the church was painted white in the 18th century.

On leaving the church, go ahead downhill through the gates. Continue into the square near the **Kings Arms Hotel**. Bear right past the front of the hotel and turn left into **Hawkshead's Main Street** immediately before the **Queens Head** pub. Take the next left to visit **Ann Tyson's House**, which is situated at the top of the street and is well worth a look.

This is where Wordsworth lodged with Hugh and Ann Tyson while at Hawkshead Grammar School. Today, it's a Grade II Listed Building run as a guesthouse. William later moved to nearby Colthouse with the Tysons in 1783.

Return to Main Street, going left past the **Red Lion Inn**. Turn left immediately after the pub on a signed right of way that follows an access road. Where this swings right, keep ahead to reach the **main road**.

arrow streets: *A typical flower-lined leyway in Hawkshead*

Cross the road and take the signed ootpath opposite. Follow a track as curves right, and then turn left on walled track to cross a **footbridge**. urn left on a footpath beside the beck. ear to the right at the first junction to ass through another gate into fields. ollow the path ahead across the field a gate. Through the gate, turn left — 's signposted to 'Loanthwaite' — and o through a kissing gate farther on. ontinue gently uphill and through a

kissing gate into an enclosed path. Turn left for about 50 metres, then turn right through a kissing gate by a large oak tree. Walk up the righthand side of the next two fields. Go through a kissing gate, and turn left along the field edge to enter a lane.

3. Turn right, up the lane signed to 'Latterbarrow', to reach a T-junction. Turn left here to reach a signed footpath for '**Latterbarrow**' on the right where the lane levels, in about 75 metres.

4. Through the gate, take the footpath to begin the climb to Latterbarrow. As

Spacious summit: *The summit of Latterbarrow offers grand views across Lakeland's southern fells*

the angle steepens, pass through trees staying left at a footpath junction. Above the trees climb more steeply and after steps, higher up, follow a grassy path to the **tall cairn** on **Latterbarrow summit**. Head left for a few metres for panoramic views over **Windermere Lake**.

5. Return to the cairn, bearing left past it to follow a good path towards forestry plantations. Just before a stile into the woods, turn right on a path signed to 'Hawkshead'. Farther down, follow the path through trees staying ahead as a path joins from the right. Shortly, after a **small footbridge**, rejoin your outbound route at a marker post and junction. Go left, following your outward route back to the lane.

Go through the gate into the lane and follow it to the access track for 'Crofts Head' and 'Croftland' on the right.

6. Turn right on the access track and bear left at a fork at **Croft Head**, taking a track through a gate. Stay on the right curving right with a hedge/fence. Pass through a gate opening going half-left past a marker post. Continue ahead to cross a stile in a wall and drop to a gate into an **enclosed footpath**.

ross over this passing through a kissing
ate a little to the right. Take the path
gned 'Hawkshead Hall/B5286' ahead,
ong the left side of the field. At a path
nction, join your outward route and

follow it back to the road at Hawkshead.
Cross over and turn left to return to the
car parks to complete the walk. ♦

Hawkshead

*Hawkshead is a pretty village that attracts huge
numbers of tourists all year round. It has a timeless
atmosphere and consists of narrow alleys, overhanging
gables and cobbled streets. William Wordsworth writes
of it in 'The Prelude'. Originally owned by the monks of
Furness Abbey, Hawkshead became an important wool
town in medieval times and was granted its first Market
Charter by King James I in 1585.*

A summer morning' on the shores of Ullswater

'Golden daffodils'

*walk beside Ullswater to Glencoyne where Wordsworth
was inspired to write his famous 'Daffodils' poem*

Distance/time: 4km/ 2½ miles. Allow 2 hours

Start/finish: Glencoyne National Trust pay and display car park
facing Glencoyne Bay

Grid ref: NY 442 112

Ordnance Survey Map: Explorer OL5 The English Lakes, North-
eastern area: *Penrith, Patterdale & Caldbeck*

After the walk: Aira Force Café, Aira Force car park, on A592 north
east of Glencoyne Bay. www.nationaltrust.org/uk/aira-force-and-
ullswater | ullswater@nationaltrust.org.uk

Walk outline

*The Ullswater shoreline is followed before a short section along
the road leads to a track and footpath that ascend Glencoyne.
A rough track is used to descend towards Ullswater passing
the cottages of 'Seldom Seen' before returning to the road. A
tree-fringed lakeside path and short road section then lead
back to the start.*

The famous 'daffodils' of Glencoyne Bay

On 15th April 1802 William Wordsworth and his sister,
Dorothy, walked along the Ullswater shore at Glencoyne
Bay, after spending the previous night in nearby Pooley
Bridge. In her Grasmere Journal, Dorothy describes the
daffodils they saw there, and, although it is not recorded,
her words almost certainly inspired William to write his
most famous poem, 'Daffodils'. Even the phraseology is
surprisingly similar.

Wordsworth loved this area and was a regular visitor to
Ullswater.

Glencoyne Farm

Wild daffodils

The Walk

1. Facing the road, leave the car park at its righthand end, taking the footpath beside the road. The footpath crosses **Glencoyne Beck** by a **footbridge** and a little farther on reaches the driveway to **Glencoyne Farm**.

2. Turn right down the access drive towards Glencoyne Farm with **Glencoyne Park** over to the right.

Glencoyne Farm is one of the largest of the National Trust's hill farms and supports a flock of more than 1,500 sheep.

Enter the **farmyard**, keeping left of barns on the waymarked path. Keep ahead to go through a gate next to the **farmhouse** and walk in front of it across the garden to leave by a small gate. Bear half-left onto an uphill path beneath telephone wires. Bend left, then right climbing steadily past occasional waymarkers with **Glencoyne Beck** below.

Pass below the cottages at '**Seldom Seen**' and continue over a beck. Immediately after the stream, bear half-left, climbing more steeply to reach a **wall** below woods.

Veer right, still climbing, now with the wall on the left, to eventually reach a corner of the wall. Bear left around the corner and go through a gate to reach the walk's **highest point**.

The view back down the valley takes in the whole of the Glencoyne valley as well as the northern half of Ullswater including the Gowbarrow shore, the site of Wordsworth's famous 'golden daffodils'.

3. Go left through a small gate and follow the path downhill through the trees beside the wall to reach the access track beyond the cottages at '**Seldom Seen**'.

Walk ahead down the track to reach the road by a bus stop.

4. Cross over and join the 'Concessionary lakeside path'. Go left, following the path above **Ullswater** lake.

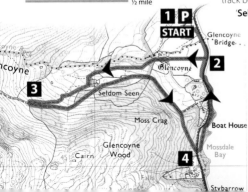

0   1km

½ mile

Above the lake: *Dropping down an old path in Glencoyne Valley towards Ullswater*

At the end of the path, cross the road taking the path opposite that runs parallel to the road. Cross the driveway to **Glencoyne Farm** and continue ahead on the path back to the car park to complete the walk.

It is worth crossing the road to access the pretty lake shore and shingle beach

It is here that Dorothy wrote, 'I never saw daffodils so beautiful, they grew among the mossy stones about and about them, some rested their heads upon these stones as on a pillow for weariness and the rest tossed and reeled and danced.' ♦

Ullswater

Arguably the most beautiful of the English Lakes, Ullswater is often compared to Switzerland's Lake Lucerne. A typical 'narrow ribbon lake' formed as glaciers gouged out the valley floor during the last Ice Age, Ullswater is the second largest of Lakeland's many lakes and meres. It measures 9 miles/14.5 kilometres long and is ¾ mile/1.2 kilometres broad at its widest point. The lake reaches depths of 197 feet/60 metres.

Cockley Beck Bridge over the River Duddon

Wm. Wordsworth

'Favourite valley'

A circuit of the River Duddon near Cockley Beck — through one of Wordsworth's favourite landscapes

Distance/time: 5.5 km/ 3½ miles. Allow 2–2½ hours

Start: Birks Bridge Forestry Commission car park and picnic area

Grid ref: SD 235 995

Ordnance Survey Map: Explorer OL6 The English Lakes, South-western area: *Coniston, Ulverston & Barrow-in-Furness*

After the walk: The Newfield Inn, Seathwaite, Duddon Valley, Broughton in Furness, LA20 6ED. www.brilliantinns.co.uk/newfield-inncumbria | 01229 716208

Walk outline

From the car park the River Duddon is crossed via a bridge and the walk goes right to follow its west bank northerly using field paths (wet in places) to Black Hall Farm. The access track is an old Roman Road that runs to the foot of the Hardknott Pass. Cockley Beck Bridge is crossed before a returning to the south via a lane along the eastern bank of the River Duddon. The final section uses fainter paths over fields.

William Wordsworth and the Duddon Valley

William Wordsworth walked almost every day, and his favourite walking area was the Duddon Valley. This is in the far south west of the National Park and is accessible by car over narrow, high passes and winding lanes. The Duddon Valley runs north from Broughton in Furness through Ulpha and Seathwaite to the Hardknott Pass, tracing the course of the River Duddon. It is sometimes called 'Dunnerdale' but Wordsworth knew it (as most do) as 'the Duddon Valley', and he wrote a sequence of thirty-five sonnets about it. An old packhorse bridge spans the river south-west of our starting point and is one of the valley's hidden gems.

River Duddon

Dipper

The Walk

1. Leave the car park, crossing the bridge over the **River Duddon**. Turn right immediately after the bridge onto a footpath marked by a blue arrow. The path is a little wet and muddy at first but soon improves, with the river over to the right.

Wordsworth loved the river Duddon and in Sonnet 1 of his River Duddon series he wrote, ' Pure flows the verse, pure, vigorous, free, and bright, For Duddon, long-loved Duddon, is my theme!'

The Duddon rises near the Three Shires Stone on the Wrynose Pass and flows for fifteen miles before entering the Irish Sea at Duddon Sands. Until 1974, the river formed the boundary between the historic counties of Lancashire and Cumberland.

The path soon improves and continues with a fence on the left.

2. Pass through a gate by a stile and continue on the opposite side of the fence (keeping it on the right) to cross a beck. Keep ahead with the river to the right.

You are deep amongst the mountains here with Harter Fell to your left, Hardknott ahead to the left, Crinkle

Crags ahead to the right, with Mosedale and Grey Friar on your right.

Continue ahead to eventually swing left with the fence and river to your right, heading towards a **gate** by trees. Go through the gate and beyond the bushes and trees go through another gate into fields again.

River song: *Walking beside the rocky River Duddon in Dunnersdale*

Keep to the righthand edge across two fenced fields, and in the third field, bear left through the centre towards **Black Hall Farm**. At a gate immediately before the farmyard, go right through a small gate taking a fence-enclosed path around the farmyard. A gate at the end of the path leads onto the farm access road.

3. Turn right down the access road, which follows the course of a minor

Roman Road. *Hardknott Roman fort is over the Hardknott Pass to your left. Dating from the Second Century AD and Emperor Hadrian's rule, the fort was called 'Mediobogdum' by the Romans.*

Follow the access road to the public road at the foot of the **Hardknott Pass**.

The Hardknott Pass is one of the steepest roads in England with gradients of 1 in 3 (33%). It rises in a series of steep and unnervingly tight bends to its summit at 1,310 feet/400 metres. There are only a few parking places at the top.

Rock and water: *Birks Bridge spans a narrow gorge on the River Duddon*

4. Turn right along the road to cross **Cockley Beck Bridge** over the **River Duddon**. Turn right at the T-junction here passing in front of **Cockley Beck Holiday Cottage**, signed for 'Broughton via The Duddon Valley'.

Walk down the lane for about 2 kilometres/1½ miles.

Pass a footpath sign for 'Black Hole' at a parking area on the right and follow the lane as it curves left towards the buildings of an **Outdoor Centre**.

5. Immediately before the buildings, go right over a stile by a gate, signed for 'The Hows'.

Head across the field following a faint path in the direction of a group of pines. Pass through a gateway and continue over the next field with a fence/wall and the River Duddon on the right. As you approach the far side of the field bear half-left, climbing to cross a stile in a wall onto the road.

Go right and, just before the road bends left and starts to drop, leave it taking a narrow path half-right. This drops back into the car park to complete the walk.

To extend the walk to the pretty **Birks Bridge**, continue down the road for about 200 metres. Cross the bridge on the right and return to the car park by the footpath on the far side of the river.

The River Duddon tumbles into a small, narrow gorge at Birks Bridge and the tiny stone bridge provides an attractive foreground to a backdrop of Lakeland's highest fells. ♦

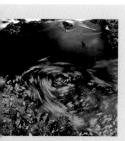

Wordsworth's river sonnets

"Still glides the stream, and shall for ever glide;
The Form remains, the Function never dies"

Wordsworth's 'The River Duddon, a series of sonnets and other poems' was written in 1820 and dedicated to his younger brother, Christopher. This collection has long been recognised as a turning point in the poet's career and an important stage in the formation of his poetic identity.

Peaceful Rydal Water, at the heart of 'Wordsworth Country'

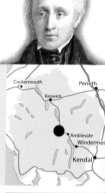

Wm. Wordsworth

'Wordsworth Country'

A memorable walk around Rydal Water and the vale of Grasmere using easy, elevated paths and tracks

Distance/time: 6km/ 4 miles. Allow 2½-3 hours. (3½ hours or more if visiting Rydal Mount)

Start: Pelter Bridge pay and display car park, off a minor road south of the A591 at the eastern end of Rydal Water and Rydal village

Grid ref: NY 364 059

Ordnance Survey Map: Explorer OL7 The English Lakes, South-eastern area: *Windermere, Kendal & Silverdale*

After the walk: The Travellers Rest, Grasmere, LA22 9RR. www.lakedistrictinns.co.uk/travellers | 015394 35604

Walk outline

A lane is followed to reach a high level track above Rydal Water. Farther on, the path drops to cross a bridge over the River Rothay near Grasmere. Next, forest tracks are followed to the A591. Across the road, a steep climb brings you to an old Coffin Road that is followed to Rydal Mount. Next we drop past Rydal Church to the A591 to visit Dora's Field before recrossing the road to climb through woodland back to the start.

'Wordsworth country'

This area is the heart of 'Wordsworth Country' and we visit Rydal Mount where Wordsworth lived from 1813 until his death in 1850. Here he wrote many of his poems, revised earlier ones and published the final version of 'Daffodils'. See: www.rydalmount.co.uk

Wordsworth family graves

We pass St Mary's Church at Rydal where William worshipped and was churchwarden from 1833 to 1834.

Dora's Field, below the church, was bought by William to build a house. But when his daughter Dora died in 1847, he planted it with hundreds of daffodils in her memory.

Rydal postbox

The Walk

1. Turn left out of the car park and walk up the gently rising lane past the entrance to **Cote How**.

Continue when the lane becomes a rough track, dropping down to pass through a gate to a fork in the track.

2. Take the lefthand fork, staying on the higher path to pass a bench on the right. **Rydal Water** is spread out below.

Follow the high-level path curving up through the woods. As the angle eases, bend right near a large **cave and quarry**. Now rise steeply, curving left and then right to reach the flooded **Rydal Cave**.

3. Pass the cave, cutting half-right with the distinctive outline of Helm Crag in the distance.

Tree covered Heron Island, visible in the lake below, was a favourite picnic spot for William and his sister, Dorothy, and they would often row out to it.

The path becomes rougher again, rising and falling with lovely views down to the lake on the right.

At a fork stay right, descending more steeply and passing a bench a little farther on. Keep left at the next fork. Rise again to join a broad path near a wall, bear left, then go ahead (the righthand fork) at a path junction. Descend beside a wall, dropping down to a **footbridge and weir**, with **Grasmere** to the left.

4. Cross the bridge into **Penny Rock Wood**. Go half right, up steps and follow the path through the woods.

0		1km
	½ mile	

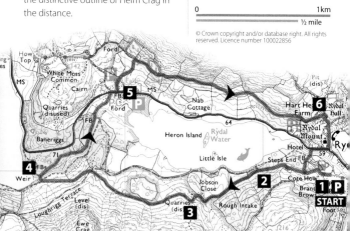

poet's home: *Wordsworth lived in Rydal* *ouse from 1813 until his death in 1850*

lose to the north west end of Rydal Water *White Moss House, the only property* *Vordsworth ever bought (he rented the* *thers) — for his son Willie. It remained in* *he Wordsworth family until the 1930s.*

o through a gate out of the woods nd follow a good path with the **River othay** over to the right. At a **foot and ycle bridge** on the right, don't cross ver, instead, bear left following the gned path for 'Car park/toilets'. Fork ft at the next junction, crossing a little

bridge to pass the **toilets**, then fork left again to reach the **A591**.

Alongside the road is a rocky outcrop with *steps cut into it known as 'Wordsworth's* *seat'. It once commanded superb views* *over Rydal Water and is said to have been* *his 'favourite view in the Lakes'.*

5. Cross the road, taking the path opposite, signed for 'Grasmere/Rydal', passing **'The Coach House'** and rising into the trees. Curve right by a **waterfall** and climb steadily on the path by a wall. Go through a gate higher up and continue climbing to reach a T-junction

Popular path: *Looking back to Rydal Water from Loughrigg Terrace*

below a house. Turn right. This path is known as the '**Old Coffin Road**'.

Coffins were carried this way for burial at St. Oswald's Church in Grasmere in the days before Rydal had its own church.

The path now contours more easily across the slopes through open woods. Ignore a right fork, rising over exposed tree roots to go through a gate and continue beside a wall. After passing through a gate in the wall corner, the path continues across more open ground.

As you approach Rydal the path is walled on both sides and you soon reach a lane near to the entrance to **Rydal Mount**.

This was Wordsworth's much-loved family home from 1813 until his death in 1850 at the age of 80. Many of his best known poems were written in the 'writing hut' in the garden, overlooking the lakes below.

6. From Rydal Mount, follow the lane right, downhill, passing **St Mary's Church**. At the A591, turn right, and in about 100 metres, you will reach **Dora's Field** on the right. *Bought originally to build a house on, the field was planted*

...ith daffodils in memory of his beloved ...aughter who died of tuberculosis in 1847.

...ontinue past Dora's Field and, just ...efore the **Badger Bar**, cross the road, ...o through a wall gap and across a

footbridge. Follow the path up the field ahead, through a kissing gate into **woods** and up to the lane used earlier in the walk. Turn left and head back to the car park to complete the walk. ♦

Wordsworth's cottage

You can visit Dove Cottage, in Grasmere, where William Wordsworth lived from 1799–1808, first with his sister, Dorothy and later with his wife, Mary. Many of his best-known earlier poems were written there. See: www.wordsworth.org.uk/visit/dove-cottage.html You can also visit St. Oswald's Church in Grasmere to see where Wordsworth and his family are buried. www. visitcumbria.com/amb/grasmere-st-oswalds-church

Wray Castle's grand Victorian Gothick portico and the croquet lawn

Beatrix's beginnings

An easy lakeside and woodland walk to Wray Castle where the young Beatrix Potter first discovered the Lake District

Distance/time: 6km/ 3½ miles. Allow 2 hours (3½ hours or more if visiting Wray Castle)

Start/finish: Red Nab National Trust car park on the west shore of Lake Windermere, south of Wray Castle

Grid ref: SD 385 994

Ordnance Survey Map: Explorer OL7 The English Lakes, South-eastern area: *Windermere, Kendal & Silverdale*

After the walk: The Drunken Duck Inn, Barngates, Ambleside, LA22 0NG. www.drunkenduckinn.co.uk | 015394 36347 | info@drunkenduckinn.co.uk

Walk outline

From the car park, a track follows the west shore of Windermere heading north. The walk continues around High Wray Bay, rising from the lake into woodland. A descent leads to a boathouse and waymarked path to Wray Castle. After a visit, the route leaves the castle past St. Margaret's Church, before heading into woodland to rejoin the outbound route along the Windermere shore.

Early Lakeland days

Beatrix Potter was sixteen when she first visited Wray Castle and the Lake District in 1882. Her family rented Wray Castle for the summer and Beatrix and her brother Bertram explored the western shore of Windermere and the tarns in the countryside beyond. It was here that Beatrix met Hardwick Rawnsley who was the vicar of Low Wray church next door. He was a regular visitor to the castle and actively involved in the preservation of the Lakeland landscape. He went on to form the National Trust with Octavia Hill and Sir Robert Hunter in 1895. Today, Wray Castle is owned by the Trust – www.nationaltrust.org.uk/wraycastle

St. Margaret's Church

Beatrix Potter with 'Spot'

The Walk

1. Facing the lake, turn left out of the car park, signed for 'Wray Castle', and follow a good track that keeps close to the lake shore on your right for about 2 kilometres/1¼ miles.

As England's largest natural lake, Windermere seemed the perfect place for wealthy Victorian industrialists to build their summer homes. Wray Castle is just one of many ostentatious period properties that were springing up around the shore.

2. At **High Wray Bay** there are two boathouses, one on each side of the little bay, and between them, a permissive path is signed through a gateway in the wall on the right.

Turn right here on the **permissive path** which keeps close to the lake shore, curving round into another little bay backed by woods. A very attractive spot

The path soon curves leftwards away from the lake. At a fork higher up, ignore the lefthand path and continue ahead to pass through a gate into woodland. Through the woods the path drops to a path junction with **Watbarrow Point** to your right through the trees.

Swing left at this junction close to the lake shore again. Pass a large black boathouse in **Low Wray Bay** and a little further on reach a path junction with a fence and fields ahead.

It is worth the short out and back detour to the wooded **Wray Crag** headland for a view to the head of the lake. For this, turn right at the junction and follow the path past the grand **Wray Castle**

0   1km

½ mile

On the water: *A Victorian stone boathouse on the Windermere shore at High Wray Bay*

Boathouse, where there is a ferry jetty, and on through the woods. Bear right to Wray Crag just before the path leaves the woods.

There are good views from this wooded headland over to Ambleside at the head of Windermere, backed by the high fells of the Fairfield Horseshoe.

Retrace your steps back past Wray Castle Boathouse to the path junction reached earlier by the fence.

3. Take the path ahead signed for 'Wray Castle' and 'Ambleside via road'. With woods on your left and a fence on your right, rise gently on a good path. As **Wray Castle** comes into view ahead, continue on the path to reach a path junction where the fence on your right bends right. Go right with the fence; it's signposted for the 'Castle'. Rise on the path to reach a road and cross it at a crossing point beneath Wray Castle. Go, left up steps, and cross another road to the entrance area for the castle and picnic benches.

Castle view: *Panoramic views from the drive take in the distant Langdale Pikes*

Beatrix Potter was 16 when her parents first rented Wray Castle for 14 weeks in the summer of 1882. It was the start of her long love affair with the Lake District. As she recorded in her secret diary, 'Had a series of adventures. Inquired the way three times, lost continually, alarmed by collies, stuck in stiles, chased by cows.'

4. Leave the Castle, and walk down the access drive, which enjoys superb views to the right to the distant Langdale Pikes. At the end of the drive, turn left along the lane.

Just past the gatehouse is the access to **St. Margaret's Church** on the left.

St. Margaret's Church at Low Wray was built at the same time as Wray Castle and often visited by the young Beatrix Potter. Its vicar, the Reverend (later Canon) Hardwicke Rawnsley, campaigned against thoughtless development in the Lake District. He later became one of the founders of the National Trust. His views had a profound effect on the young Beatrix, who came to love this landscape and later bequeathed all her Cumbrian farms and other properties to the Trust.

5. Immediately after the access to the

church, turn left on a path signed 'Cycle path' and 'Bowness via Ferry'. Walk down the track with an old wall on the left. Descend gradually (mostly in trees) to reach a path junction with a gate in the wall on the left were you re-join your outward route. Follow the shore path back to the car park at **Red Nab** to complete the walk. ♦

Wray Castle

Wray Castle was built in 1840 by James Dawson, a retired Liverpool surgeon whose wife, Margaret, inherited a large fortune from her father. The Castle was built in a mock-Gothic fantasy style with lofty halls, castellated walls and fairytale towers. This was the height of fashion in Victorian times. The intention was both to impress guests and demonstrate the owner's immense wealth and social standing.

Virginia creeper covers the front of Lingholm house

Beatrix Potter

Summer inspiration

A woodland walk near Derwentwater to Lingholm and Fawe Park where Beatrix Potter spent her childhood holidays

Distance/time: 5km/ 3 miles. Allow 1½-2 hours

Start/finish: Small free car park at northern end of Catbells, on the minor lane signed to 'Skelgill', beside Gutherscale Lodge.

Grid ref: NY 245 210

Ordnance Survey Map: Explorer OL4 The English Lakes, North-western area: *Keswick, Cockermouth & Wigton*

After the walk: Chalet Restaurant and Tearooms, Portinscale, Keswick, CA12 5RF. www.thechaletportinscale.co.uk | 017687 72757 infor@thechaletportinscale.co.uk

Walk outline

This is a walk along forest tracks and paths. The route is easy to follow but there are a few steep ups and downs that may be slippery after rain. The walk heads north past Lingholm to reach Derwentwater at Nichol End Marina. It returns past Fawe Park to rejoin the outbound route back to the car park.

Holidays in North Lakeland

Beatrix Potter's family rented Wray Castle (see Walk 6) for just one summer before they turned their attention to North Lakeland. When Beatrix was nineteen, in 1885, the family rented a large house called Lingholm near the western shore of Derwentwater. And for the next six summers up until 1891, the family holidayed there every summer. (See www.thelingholmestate.co.uk for modern lettings). Later, they took Fawe Park, next door, for a year.

Lingholm entrance sign

These were formative trips for the young Beatrix who used her time at Lingholm and Fawe Park to sketch animals and local scenes. *The Tale of Squirrel Nutkin* was born here. Owl Island, which features in the book, was also based on St Herbert's Island in Derwentwater.

Red squirrel

The Walk

1. Leave the car park and head right along the lane. Bear left at the road junction, cross the cattle grid and on the sharp left-hand bend take the footpath ahead for '**Keswick, Brandelhow & Hawse End Launch Pier**'. Follow the descending woodland path to a **lane**. Go half-left over the lane to a footpath signed to 'Portinscale'. Follow the path through the woods to cross a footbridge and kissing gate.

2. Walk across an open area and go through another gate to re-enter woodland. Rise gently and continue, soon with a fence on the right.

Cross the drive for **Lingholm**, taking the signposted 'Footpath to Keswick'.

Lingholm was built in the 1870s but was often empty or rented out. The Potters spent several happy summers here in the 1890s. Beatrix later painted the backgrounds for her Tale of Squirrel Nutkin *and* Tale of Mrs Tiggy-Winkle *in the gardens.*

Follow the woodland track to a junction of paths on a bend where the main path swings right.

3. Walk ahead (off the main path), uphill through the trees. The path rises more steeply, then levels out before dropping steeply to reach a road.

Go onto the road through a gap in the hedge and turn right. Walk along the road to the entrance to **Nichol End Marina**.

4. Turn right down the access road passing the entrance to **Fawe Park** on the right. Walk past the shop and café to reach the shores of **Derwent Water**.

5. Retrace your steps for a few metres and turn left up behind the **café** and **marina shop**. Cross a tarmac drive by **The Lodge** and follow the footpath/track ahead alongside the boundary wall of **Fawe Park**.

Jetty set: *Nichol End Marina at the northern end of Derwentwater*

The Potter family spent a single summer at Fawe Park in 1885. Beatrix sketched many of the details for her watercolour illustrations in The Tale of Benjamin Bunny *in the walled kitchen garden here. As she wrote to her publisher, Frederick Warne, 'I have done every imaginable rabbit background and miscellaneous sketches as well — about 70!'*

As the track levels it curves right to rise up and rejoin your outward route at the track junction by a forest barrier. Curve left, pass the entrance to Lingholm again, and follow your outward route back to your car to complete the walk. ♦

Where the National Trust began
The National Trust was formed on 12th January 1895 by Canon Hardwick Rawnsley, Sir Robert Hunter and Octavia Hill. In the early days it was concerned with the protection of open spaces but as time passed its aims became specifically 'the preservation for the benefit of the nation of lands and tenements of beauty or historic interest'. The first places it protected were White Barrow on Salisbury Plain and Wicken Fen, in Cambridgeshire.

Relaxing at Skelgill Farm

Beatrix Potter

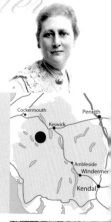

Newland connections

An energetic circuit in the Newlands Valley exploring the western flank of Catbells — the home of Mrs Tiggy-Winkle

Distance/time: 5km/ 3 miles. Allow 2-2½ hours

Start: Parking area with honesty box at Chapel Bridge near Newlands Church, south west of Little Town

Grid ref: NY 231 194

Ordnance Survey Map: Explorer OL4 The English Lakes, North-western area: *Keswick, Cockermouth & Wigton*

After the walk: The Farmers Arms, Portinscale, Near Keswick, CA12 6RW. www.marstonpubs.co.uk/thefarmersarms | 017687 772322

Walk outline

A steep lane climbs from the car park towards Little Town. A rough fell path then ascends the lower reaches of Yewthwaite Combe, before Yewthwaite Gill is crossed at old mine workings. The route traces a high level track under the western slopes of Catbells before dropping to Skelgill Farm. From here field paths and tracks descend to Little Town where a short section of lane takes us back to the car park.

Valley of inspiration

The Tale of Mrs Tiggy-Winkle is unique because Beatrix Potter set it wholly in a real place. Potter based her eponymous heroine on a Scottish washerwoman called Kitty MacDonald, while Mrs Tiggy-Winkle was a pet hedgehog that Beatrix had brought with her on holiday.

Many of the places illustrated in the book, such as Skelgill Farm and Little Town, are visited on this walk. Mrs Tiggy-Winkle's cottage was set at the 'back of Catbells'. The fictional Lucie who comes to tea was based on Lucie Carr, the daughter of the Vicar of Newland's church. In fact, the book was dedicated to her and published in October 1905.

Newlands church

Hedgehog

The Walk

1. Leave the car park and turn right up the lane. Follow the lane steadily uphill for about 400 metres to reach **Little Town** — a handful of farms and cottages. Immediately before the first farm on the left, turn sharp right, off the lane onto a **bridleway**. Go through a large gate and pass above a cottage down to the right.

2. The track turns sharp left and then keeps close to walled fields on the left, heading towards the slopes of **Catbells**.

Beatrix Potter developed the Tale of Mrs Tiggy-Winkle while holidaying at Lingholm in 1901. She already knew Catbells well from her earlier childhood adventures (see Walk 7). The illustrations of the Newlands Valley and the path above Little Town that appeared in the published book come straight from her sketchbook.

Continue on the broad path close to the wall heading towards old mine workings.

The small door to Mrs Tiggy-Winkle's house that Lucie finds beneath a rock on the hillside was based on the real timber doors once used to block off abandoned mine shafts on the fells.

Stay on the main path keeping with the wall and ignoring minor paths off to the right. Take care with children around the workings.

3. As you near the mines the path curves right to cross a footbridge over **Yewthwaite Gill**. Once over, the path swings left between spoil heaps to run beside the wall again. At the end of the mine workings the track continues, still

Into the valley: *Crossing fields between Skelgill and Little Town in the Newlands Valley*

...beside the wall on the left and with superb views of the **Newlands Valley** to your left and behind.

The Newlands Valley is probably one of the most picturesque of all Lakeland valleys and was a favourite of Beatrix Potter. During here explorations for The Tale of Mrs Tiggy-Winkle , she visited Skelghyl, Little Town and other sheep farms on the fells. When published, the book was generously dedicated to 'The real little Lucie of Newlands'.

Follow the track until it eventually starts to descend and the wall on the left becomes a fence, and later on, after a gate, becomes a wall again. As the track ends, pass a barrier (near a sign for 'Yewthwaite') to reach a lane.

4. Turn sharp left, passing through a gate to **Skelgill Farm**. Follow the lane as it curves right down past the farmhouse. Immediately after the farmhouse (spring and well in the wall on the left), turn left and go through a gate by the 'Skelgill Farm' sign.

Green vale: *Little Town sits in the green bowl of the Newlands Valley*

Follow the path through trees, which frame superb views up the valley to Hindscarth and Robinson, and out into fields.

The path continues ahead passing through fenced fields with stiles and gates. After a gate in a stone wall, the path is less obvious but follows a line of hawthorn bushes, first on the left, then the right.

The path soon becomes clearer again and after a few more fields passes a **house** on the right.

After a gate, the path follows a farm track. Continue along the track, which becomes enclosed a little further on, eventually curving left to cross a footbridge over a small brook.

5. After the footbridge, go through a gate and turn right to reach a lane. Turn left along the lane to pass through **Little Town**.

The first picture in the book shows whitewashed Little Town Farm and its farmyard although, for artistic reasons, Beatrix has transposed the Skelghyl farmhouse to Little Town. Many of the book's backgrounds are recognisable in the Newlands valley, too; notably

...ne illustrating the story when 'Lucie
...rambled up the hill as fast as her stout
...gs would carry her; she ran along a
...eep path-way — up and up — until
...ttle-town was right away down below.'

Follow the descending lane beyond Little
Town back to the car park to complete
the walk. ♦

From writer to shepherd?

*Beatrix Potter published her first book, 'The Tale of Peter
Rabbit', privately in 1901. Publishers Frederick Warne &
Co soon took it up and Beatrix used the profits from her
books (plus an inherited legacy) to buy Hill Top Farm
at Near Sawrey (see Walk 10). She eventually published
twenty-three books but, after marrying Hawkshead
solicitor William Heelis, her main interests changed to
breeding Herdwick sheep and landscape conservation.*

The Tongue with Beatrix Potter's Troutbeck Park Farm at its foot

Beatrix Potter

Sheep farming days

Visit Troutbeck Park Farm which Beatrix Potter bought and where she met her friend and shepherd Tom Storey

Distance/time: 5.5km/ 3½ miles. Allow 2 hours

Start/finish: Small lay-by on the west side of the Kirkstone Pass road (A592). Just north of the Queens Head Hotel and road junction

Grid ref: NY 415 039

Ordnance Survey Map: Explorer OL7 The English Lakes, South-eastern area: *Windermere, Kendal & Silverdale*

After the walk: Queens Head Hotel, Townhead, Troutbeck, LA23 ?W. www.queensheadtroutbeck.co.uk | 015394 32174 | reservations@queensheadtroutbeck.co.uk

Walk outline

The route heads down the Kirkstone Pass road (A592) to drop through the hamlet of Town Head. Beyond this we follow Ing Lane (access drive for Troutbeck Park Farm). This heads north, crossing Trout Beck at Ing Bridge and again at Hagg Bridge. A footpath climbs past Troutbeck Park Farm to join a track that turns westwards behind the farm. Another track then returns past the farm to rejoin the outward route at Hagg Bridge.

Farm buying and sheep farming

Beatrix Potter was 47 years old when she became Mrs Heelis. Although she kept writing, her interests turned increasingly to sheep farming and Lakeland conservation. After buying Hill Top Farm at Near Sawrey, Beatrix quickly acquired three other nearby farms to help protect her own land. She continued to buy land for the next half century and became a respected breeder of the traditional Lakeland Herdwick sheep. One of the first large purchases she made was Troutbeck Park Farm in 1923. It was here that she first met her trusted friend and shepherd Tom Storey.

Troutbeck church

Herdwick ram

The Walk

1. Walk back down the A592 (Kirkstone Pass road) towards the **Queens Head Hotel**. Pass a sign for **The Mortal Man** pub and in a few more metres leave the main road, taking a minor lane off to the left. Descend past cottages at **Town Head** to a point where the lane bends right and starts climbing again at a junction.

2. Turn left here, along the lane dropping into the Troutbeck valley. As it levels out, follow the lane — **Ings Lane** — along the flat floor of the valley.

Just a few hundred feet above, the busy Kirkstone Pass road takes traffic over the pass to Glenridding and Ullswater, but here in the valley bottom you are hardly aware of it. It is easy to see why Beatrix Potter was attracted to this peaceful valley head amongst the eastern fells.

3. Cross **Ings Bridge** about half way along the valley and pass the access drive to '**Long Green Head Farm**' continuing on towards **Troutbeck Tongue**, ahead.

In the Lakes, a 'tongue' refers to a wedge of high or rising ground usually enclosed between becks. One of the most distinctive 'tongues' in

the region is Troutbeck Tongue. The view of the Troutbeck valley from the top is magnificent.

Afternoon light: *Troutbeck Park Farm from the slopes of Troutbeck Tongue*

4. Almost at the end of the valley, go through a large gate across the lane and in about 75 metres, immediately after the insignificant **Hagg Bridge** over the beck, turn right off the lane at a stile and footpath signed for 'High Street'.

The path heads over a grassy a field with **Hagg Gill** over to the right. Climb more steeply now to a wall and go through a kissing gate onto a track signed for 'Troutbeck Village'.

5. Turn left on the rough, stony track descending towards **Troutbeck Park Farm** ahead.

When Beatrix Potter bought Troutbeck Park Farm it was her biggest purchase so far. It took time and a lot of hard work to get the farm in good working order. After this she always bought larger estates and properties; her grandest purchase was in 1930 when she acquired the Monk Coniston Estate. This covered four thousand acres between Little Langdale and Coniston and included the two well known Lakeland farms of High Yewdale

Herdwick home: *Beatrix Potter bred Herdwick sheep at Troutbeck Park Farm*

and Tilberthwaite. Troutbeck Park Farm is now a National Trust Property.

Before you reach the farm and just before a gate ahead; leave the track going right for a few metres beside a wall, then go left through a gate in the wall. Continue ahead along the left edge of a sloping field with a wall to the left and Troutbeck Park Farm below.

Pass through another gate in the far wall and drop to join a farm track. Turn left towards the farm.

6. Go through a gate to the right of the farm outbuildings and turn left past barns and towards the front of the farmhouse. Follow the access road away from the farm.

Once Beatrix Potter had bought Troutbeck Park Farm, her flocks of Herdwick sheep grew significantly and she needed expert help to manage them and run the farm. A shepherd called Tom Storey was highly regarded in the area and Beatrix was able to hire him. They worked together well and Beatrix was so pleased with Tom that she paid him a handsome wage to move to her Hill Top Farm in Sawrey.

She later also employed George Walker, Tom Storey's brother-in-law, to help with

the running of Troutbeck Park Farm. Tom worked for Beatrix for another eighteen years and she left him £400 in her will and instructed that, although Hill Top was to go to the National Trust, Tom was to take over the tenancy.

The farm access road meets Ings Lane near Hagg Bridge. Follow the lane back along the valley to Town Head bearing right up to the A592. Turn right up the road to complete the walk. ◆

Herdwick sheep

Herdwick sheep are native to the Lake District and noted for their toughness and the warmth of their wool. Beatrix Potter became a noted breeder of these hardy sheep, and won many prizes between 1930 and 1938. As well as breeding Herdwicks, she judged them at agricultural shows. On her death, she bequeathed fifteen farms and more than 4,000 acres to the National Trust. Every one of the farms still grazes her beloved Herdwick sheep.

A pink sunset reflected in the still waters of Moss Eccles Tarn

'Beatrix Potter Country'

A walk around 'Beatrix Potter Country' taking in Hill Top Farm and the tarns around Claife Heights

Distance/time: 6km/ 4 miles. Allow 2½-3 hours (or 3½ hours if visiting Hill Top)

Start/finish: Braithwaite Hall honesty box car park, facing Cuckoo Brow in Far Sawrey. The Hall is just south of The Cuckoo Brow Inn

Grid ref: SD 378 954

Ordnance Survey Map: Explorer OL7 The English Lakes, South-eastern area: *Windermere, Kendal & Silverdale*

After the walk: Cuckoo Brow Inn, Far Sawrey, Ambleside, LA22 0LQ. www.cuckoobrow.co.uk | 015394 43425 | stay@cuckoobrow.co.uk

Walk outline

From Far Sawrey the route follows a quiet lane and then a track up to Moss Eccles Tarn. We continue northerly on the track reaching our farthest point at Wise Een Tarn. We return the same way but branch south-westwards at a fork to descend on a track to Near Sawrey with an optional (paid) visit to Hill Top Farm. A new path from Near Sawrey means there's only a short section of lane to return to the start.

Hill Top Farm

Hill Top was purchased by Beatrix Potter in 1905 with proceeds from her early books and a small inheritance from an aunt. She also bought the accompanying 34 acre working farm. She intended to use it as her home away from London and as an artistic retreat. The house, farm and village of Near Sawrey appear in many of Beatrix's books including *The Tale of the Pie and The Patty-Pan*, *The Tale of Tom Kitten*, *The Tale of Jemima Puddle-Duck* and *The Tale of Samuel Whiskers*. When Beatrix married William Heelis in October 1913, she left Hill Top to live at Castle Cottage on Castle Farm. See: www.nationaltrust.org.uk/hill-top

National Trust sign

Waterlilies

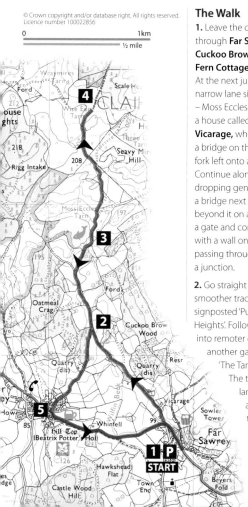

The Walk

1. Leave the car park and go left through **Far Sawrey**, passing the **Cuckoo Brow Inn**. Walk downhill past **Fern Cottage** and two lanes on the left. At the next junction, turn right onto a narrow lane signed, 'Public Bridleway – Moss Eccles Tarn'. Walk uphill to pass a house called **The Glen** and the **Old Vicarage,** where the lane levels out. At a bridge on the left, leave the lane to fork left onto a waymarked bridleway. Continue alongside **Wilfin Beck**, dropping gently, to cross the beck by a bridge next to a ford. Continue uphill beyond it on a rough track. Go through a gate and continue up the sunken track with a wall on the left. Stay on the track passing through another gate to reach a junction.

2. Go straight ahead here on the smoother track, through a gate. It's signposted 'Public Bridleway – Claife Heights'. Follow the walled track to rise into remoter countryside. Go through another gate passing a sign for 'The Tarns' and 'Claife Heights'. The track climbs into a wilder landscape, crosses a stream, and continues past a dam to a clump of trees at **Moss Eccles Tarn**.

The countryside around here was an area Beatrix Potter knew and loved to

Frog pond?: *Moss Eccles Tarn was the setting for several of Beatrix Potter's tales*

explore. Moss Eccles Tarn is reputed to have provided her with the inspiration for her book The Tale of Jeremy Fisher. *The tarn is man-made and five acres in extent. It is now owned by the National Trust.*

3. Continue to the right of Moss Eccles Tarn and follow the winding track gently uphill into lovely, wild country. Go through a gate in a wall, and you will see **Wise Een Tarn**, below and to your left. It's backed by great views of the

Langdale and Coniston Fells. Continue along the track to a point just before it drops down towards another tarn on the right. It's an ideal spot for a lunch break on a nice day.

Wise Een Tarn is set in a remote location and is notable for its rich aquatic life and numerous birds.

Ahead and to your right is the undulating, wooded hill of Claife Heights, which rises to about 900 feet/274 metres. It is around here that Beatrix Potter's ashes are said to have been scattered by her old friend and shepherd, Tom Storey.

Lake view: *Wise Een Tarn overlooks the Langdale Pikes, Crinkle Crags and Bow Fell*

4. Retrace your steps back from the tarn passing through the gate in the wall to return on the track past **Moss Eccles Tarn**. Continue on the outbound route, crossing the stream below the dam wall and continuing to pass through a gate. Beyond a gate/opening reach the track junction again and here, leave your outbound route to fork right on a track and go through a gate. Follow the tree lined track past a barn left. Exit the trees to pass through a gate and continue past another barn (on the right). Follow

the track to drop into **Near Sawrey**, passing between pretty cottages and houses to reach the road facing an **old post box**. If you have tickets for Hill Top you can turn left here and walk past the **Tar Barn Arms** to go right into the house after the second bus stop.

If you intend to visit Hill Top and have not bought tickets already, you will need to go right and then left into Hill Top car park where the ticket office is. Once armed with tickets, return to the post box and continue ahead, as above.

5. Once you have visited **Hill Top Farm**, leave the property and turn right along

he road. Go right, through a gate, and
..en shortly turn left and follow a path
..gned to 'Ferry via Far Sawrey'. Beyond
.. gate, leave the path to go left over a
..ridge and pass through a kissing gate

to the road. Go right, along the road,
taking care as it can be busy, back to **Far
Sawrey** and the car park to complete
the walk. ♦

At rest in the hills

*Beatrix Potter died on 22nd December 1943 aged 77.
She left instructions with her friend and shepherd, Tom
Storey, about where to put her ashes. He took them to
a secret location on Claife Heights where he scattered
them as he had promised. He told nobody where they
were but when he became ill in later life, he is said to
have shared the secret with his son.*

Useful Information

Cumbria Tourism
Cumbria Tourism's official website covers everything from accommodation and events to attractions and adventure. **www.golakes.co.uk**

Lake District National Park
The Lake District National Park website also has information on things to see and do, plus maps, webcams and news. **www.lakedistrict.gov.uk**

Tourist Information Centres
The main TICs provide free information on everything from accommodation and travel to what's on and walking advice.

Ambleside	01539 432 582	tic@thehubofambleside.com
Bowness	01539 442 895	bownesstic@lake-district.gov.uk
Coniston	01539 441 533	mail@conistontic.org
Keswick	01768 772 645	keswicktic@lake-district.gov.uk
Penrith	01768 867 466	pen.tic@eden.gov.uk
Ullswater	01768 482 414	ullswatertic@lake-district.gov.uk
Windermere	01539 446 499	windermeretic@southlakeland.gov.uk

Places to visit
Wordsworth House, Main Street, Cockermouth, CA13 9RX. Birthplace of William **Wordsworth** and sister Dorothy. 01900 824805 | www.nationaltrust.org.uk/wordsworth-house/

Grammar School, Hawkshead, LA22 0QF. **Wordsworth**'s old school. 015394 36735 | www.hawksheadgrammar.org.uk

Dove Cottage, Grasmere, LA22 9SH. **Wordsworth**'s home from 1799 to 1808. 015394 3554 | https://wordsworth.org.uk/visit/dove-cottage.html

Wray Castle, Low Wray, Ambleside, LA22 0JA. **Beatrix Potter**'s influential first Lake District holiday home. 015394 33250 | www.nationaltrust.org.uk/wray-castle/

Hill Top Farm, Near Sawrey, Ambleside, LA22 0LF. **Beatrix Potter**'s first house in the Lake District. 015394 36269 | www.nationaltrust.org.uk/hill-top

Beatrix Potter Gallery, Main Street, Hawkshead, LA22 0NS. **Beatrix Potter**'s original artwork 015394 36355 | www.nationaltrust.org.uk/beatrixpottergallery

World of Beatrix Potter Attraction, Bowness on Windermere, LA23 3BX. Exhibition bringing **Beatrix Potter**'s characters to life. 0844 504 1233 | www.hop-skip-jump.com

Weather
Five day forecast for the Lake District
0844 846 2444   **www.lakedistrict.gov.uk/weatherline**